GREEN PLANET

by Moira Butterfield • Illustrated by Jonathan Woodward

To Ian, Jack, and Gus, always ~ M.B.

For Mali and Samson, my two creative, nature-loving cubs.
May your world always be full of wonder ~ J.W.

360 DEGREES, an imprint of Tiger Tales
5 River Road, Suite 128, Wilton, CT 06897
First published in the United States 2018
Text by Moira Butterfield
Illustrations by Jonathan Woodward
Text and illustrations copyright © 2018 Little Tiger Press Ltd.
ISBN-13: 978-1-944530-97-6
ISBN-10: 1-944530-97-5
Printed in China
LT/1800/0097/0720

For more insight and activities, visit us at www.tigertalesbooks.com

The Forest Stewardship Council® (FSC®) is an international,
non-governmental organization dedicated to promoting responsible
management of the world's forests. FSC® operates a system of forest
certification and product labeling that allows consumers to identify
wood and wood-based products from well-managed forests and other sources.

For more information about the FSC®, please visit their website at www.fsc.org

Contents

Our Green Planet

The next time you go out for a walk, look at the trees around you. Every single tree helps to support life on Earth. Trees make snug homes for billions of creatures, trees create oxygen to help us breathe, and trees even help us make paper, just like the pages in this book.

Fabulous Forests

This is a map of the world with its forests colored green.

North America

Eurasia

Africa

South America

Oceania

Leafy Lodges

More animals live in our forests than anywhere else on Earth. Our forests are home to more than 50% of the world's plant and animal population.

Lots of Leaves

There are roughly 5 trillion trees in the world—more trees than you would be able to count in a lifetime!

Tropical Rain Forests

Tropical rain forests are thick and full of trees. They grow around the Equator—the middle of the world—where the weather is warm all year round and there is a lot of rain.

macaw

The rain forest is a great place to see incredible creatures, such as brightly-colored parrots and noisy monkeys.

lion tamarin

green woodpecker

Temperate Forests

Temperate forests grow in cooler parts of the world and have changing seasons—spring, summer, autumn, and winter. Some of the trees have leaves that change color and drop off in winter.

Creatures that live in temperate forests need to adapt to the changing seasons.

Boreal Forests

wolf

Boreal forests grow all across the far north of the world, where it gets very cold in winter. Most boreal trees have needles instead of flat leaves. The needles don't drop off in winter.

A boreal forest is a great place to find insects in the summer. In the winter, you might see animal tracks in the snow around the trees.

A Living Tree

Imagine a tree standing in the middle of a deep-green forest. It needs to be strong enough to stand tall in the face of wind, rain, sun, or snow. Now imagine all the creatures living among its branches: birds, butterflies, and many more!

Thick Skin

Bark protects a tree from damage. What the bark looks like depends on the tree. It might be as smooth as a polished table or as knobbly and rough as a crocodile's skin.

Perfect Peeler

Tree bark cracks open or peels off as a tree grows bigger. New bark grows underneath.

Ring Around

A tree grows a new tree ring every year. Each ring has a pale part and a dark part. The pale part grows in spring. The dark part grows in summer.

Thirsty Roots

Trees drink water from underground. Water travels up inside a tree through its roots and reaches the leaves through tiny veins.

Sticky Sap

Trees make a sticky liquid called sap. Sap contains chemicals to help protect the tree from diseases and insect attacks.

Yummy Maple

MAPLE SYRUP

Some sap is poisonous, so it's best not to touch it. However, people do eat the delicious, edible sap of the maple tree.

Stand Tall

A very strong layer called heartwood runs up through the middle of a tree. It keeps the tree standing.

Extreme Trees

Trees can be mighty green giants, as tall as buildings, or teeny-tiny shoots, smaller than your little finger. They can even live for thousands of years. Take a look at some of the most amazing trees of all.

Widest

Baobabs are the world's fattest trees. They grow in parts of southern Africa, and the widest ones measure more than 30 feet (10 m) around.

baobab

Tallest

Giant redwoods are the tallest trees of all. The highest ones on Earth are found growing in part of California in the United States. They reach up more than 295 feet (90 m)—as high as a multistory building.

giant redwood

Oldest

The oldest trees in the world are the Great Basin bristlecone pines that grow in the mountains of the northwestern United States. The oldest one so far discovered is more than 5000 years old. It began growing when human civilization was only just beginning.

Great Basin bristlecone pine

empress foxglove

An empress foxglove could grow this much in a day!

0.5 inch (1.4 cm)

Fastest

The world's fastest-growing tree is the empress foxglove. It can grow as much as 12 inches (30 cm) in just three weeks. That's about the height of this book!

How big is big?

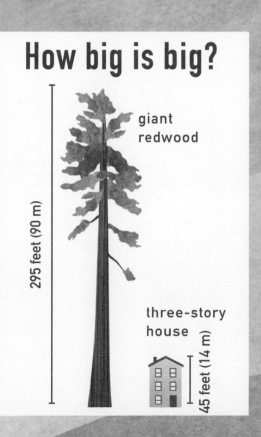

giant redwood

295 feet (90 m)

three-story house

45 feet (14 m)

Tiniest

The tiniest tree on Earth is the dwarf willow, which grows in the chilly far-north of the world. The smallest dwarf willows are only around 0.6 inch (1.6 cm) tall.

dwarf willow

3 feet (1 m)

How Do Trees Eat?

Just like you, a tree needs food to grow and stay healthy. It makes its own food using its leaves. Leaves are incredible food-making factories!

1 Leaves contain a green substance called chlorophyll (clor-oh-fil). It's the reason that our forests are so green! The chlorophyll soaks up sunlight.

2 Leaves contain water, and they are covered in tiny holes called stomata. The holes soak up a gas called carbon dioxide from the air.

3 Leaves use sunlight energy to change water and carbon dioxide into sugar and into a gas called oxygen.

4 The tree uses the sugar as food. The oxygen goes back out through the leaves into the air.

Leaves keep a tree alive, but they're also useful for many creatures. They provide food and a good hiding place.

dusky leaf monkey

The dusky leaf monkey from Malaysia, like a lot of monkeys, likes to eat tree leaves.

The red-eyed tree frog from Central America sleeps with its sticky toes stuck to the bottom of a leaf. It's a great hiding place.

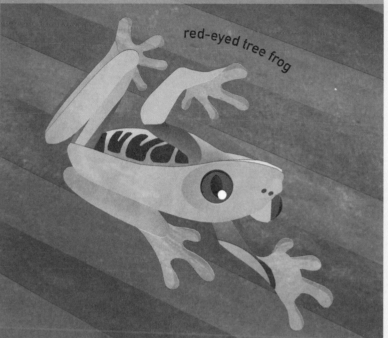

red-eyed tree frog

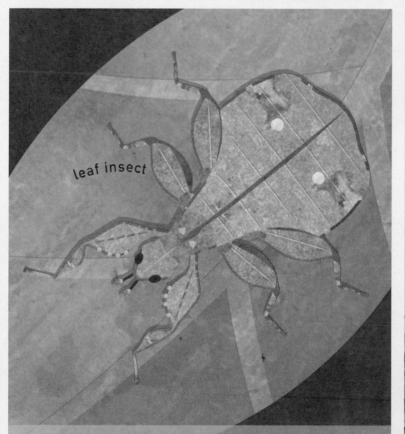

leaf insect

The leaf insect from Asia and Australia looks like a green leaf, which helps it to hide from its enemies.

The northern goshawk from Europe uses fresh, white pine leaves in its nest because they contain chemicals that keep insects away. Many different hawks do this.

northern goshawk

Forests of Snow

The boreal forests stretch for mile after mile across the north of the planet. Sometimes the fir trees that grow there are draped in snow. Here are just a few of the creatures who hide in this winter wonderland.

moose

Massive Moose

Moose like to bathe in the forest ponds, munching on pondweed. Male moose grow giant antlers up to 6 feet (1.8 m) wide.

wood frog

Frozen Frog

One of the most amazing creatures in the boreal forest is the wood frog. It can survive for several weeks frozen solid. When it thaws out, it hops away as if nothing happened!

lynx

Eager Eagles

Eagles swoop down over the trees to grab tasty animals in their sharp talons. A bald eagle's outstretched wings can measure up to 6.5 feet (2 m) wide.

bald eagle

Cunning Cats

Lynx creep on their soft, silent paws, hoping to pounce on a creature to eat.

wolf

Wolf Pack

Wolves can travel more than ten miles a day in search of food to eat. They hunt for animals like moose or deer.

snowshoe hare

Hidden Hares

Small creatures, such as snowshoe hares, scuttle around beneath the trees. The hares have a clever winter trick: their brown fur turns white to help them hide in the snow.

13

There's a Bear!

Bears have long claws, giant paws, and sharp teeth, and they're definitely not cuddly! Bears live in the boreal forest, and the biggest of all are the grizzly bears.

grizzly bear

Big and Small

An adult male grizzly bear is taller than a man when it stands on its hind legs. A newborn grizzly bear cub is tiny — it's about the size of a rat.

Grizzly Guzzlers

Grizzlies will eat any type of food, including plants, and animals such as fish and insects. It's true that they like to eat honey, but they also munch on the bees they find, too!

Quick, Run!

Grizzlies are peaceful unless they feel threatened. Then they charge! Grizzlies can run much faster than a human over a short distance.

Giant Claws

A grizzly bear's front claws can grow up to 4 inches (10 cm) long.

Sleeping Bears

Bears, such as grizzlies, hibernate in winter, sleeping through the cold months, hidden away in dens that they have dug. They come out again in spring.

Double Cubs

Female bears sometimes give birth during the winter. They usually have twins.

Baby Bears

The babies are born without fur or teeth. During the winter, they feed on their mother's milk and grow big enough to come outside in spring.

Big Bears

The cubs will stay with their mom for two or three years, until they are big enough to live on their own.

Fir Forest Bugs

Thousands of tiny creatures live in and around the fir trees of the boreal forest. There is so much to explore on the Canadian forest floor.

carpenter ant

ground beetle

Chewy Chambers

Carpenter ants make their nests in dead wood. They chew up the crumbly wood to make nest chambers.

Ground Hunter

There are many different types of ground beetle. They have wings, but most of them don't fly. They crawl around hunting for other creatures.

mayfly

From Water to Sky

Mayflies are born as little underwater creatures in forest ponds or swamps. Eventually they leave the water and turn into flies.

bee

Pouncing Predator

Wolf spiders don't spin webs. Instead they hide, waiting to pounce on their prey.

wolf spider

Bright-eyed

There are many summertime moths and butterflies in the boreal forest. This luna moth has bright eyespots on its wings to scare off birds who might want to eat it.

white-spotted longhorn beetle

luna moth

Toasted Treat

White-spotted longhorn beetles chew up dead wood. Their favorite treat is wood that has been burned!

Forests of Steam

The rain forests of the world grow around the middle of the planet. They are damp, hot, and thick with trees. The biggest rain forest is the Amazon, which grows across South America. It is home to thousands of different types of animals, as well as the giant Amazon River.

jaguar

Prowling Pouncer

The rare and beautiful jaguar prowls the Amazon. Its name means "kills with one leap." It catches its meals by hiding in a tree and jumping down onto passing animals.

black caiman

Deadly Black

The caiman is a smaller cousin of the alligator. The black caiman can grow as big as 15 feet (4.5 m)—about as long as a cargo van.

Sloth

The two-toed sloth uses its long, hooked claws to hang from a branch. It lives its entire life in trees and even sleeps hanging upside down. It spends its days munching leaves . . . very, v-e-r-y slowly.

two-toed sloth

Giant Raptor

Trees in the Amazon grow as high as multistory buildings, and the tallest of the them are home to giant harpy eagles. They sit on their treetop nests, watching the forest below. Then they swoop down to grab monkeys and birds to eat.

harpy eagle

Monkey

The rain forest can be a noisy place, with birds calling and monkeys chattering. Howler monkeys are the loudest of all. They make a scary, roaring sound in their throat, which inflates like a bag being filled with air.

howler monkey

Big Squeeze

The world's largest snake, the anaconda, likes to hide underwater by the rain forest riverbank, waiting for its prey. It can grow to around 20 feet (6 m) long—that's half as long as a bus. It winds itself around its prey and squeezes tightly.

anaconda

Monkey Business

If you are lucky enough to visit the Amazon rain forest, you might catch a glimpse of a little spider monkey swinging above your head, like a fantastic circus acrobat doing unbelievable tricks in the trees.

Twirly Tails

A spider monkey can wrap the tip of its tail around a tree branch. It can wrap its big toe around, too, like a finger.

Monkey Swings

Sometimes the spider monkeys swing on lianas, which look like ropes draped from the trees. They are actually plants growing up from the ground.

liana

Forest Food

The rain forest trees are full of delicious food for the monkeys. They spend their days looking for fruit, berries, eggs, leaves, and insects.

Monkey Talk

The monkeys live together in a big group. They call to each other through the forest, making screeching and barking noises.

Baby Steps

Babies cling onto their moms for a few weeks until they are big enough to gradually start moving around by themselves.

Playful Pouncers

Once the babies are old enough, they begin to play with other young monkeys, chasing and jumping between branches.

Snuggle Up

A group of spider monkeys will rest together in a sleeping tree, hidden high above the ground and safe from predators.

spider monkey

Rain Forest Stars

The Amazon rain forest is home to the most remarkable creatures. There are deadly frogs, super-strong beetles, and butterflies the size of cereal bowls!

Fungus Farmers

Leafcutter ants are tiny forest gardeners. They cut off slices of leaf and carry the pieces back to their nest, where they chew them up to make a mushy pulp. They grow fungus on the leaf pulp, then eat the fungus crop they have grown.

leafcutter ant

Supersized Spider

The goliath bird-eating spider is the biggest spider in the world. Its legs can grow up to 12 inches (30 cm) long, and its body can grow as big as a grown-up's fist. It crawls around the rain forest floor, hunting for small animals to eat.

goliath bird-eating spider

Snack Attack!

The praying mantis is cleverly disguised to look like part of a plant. It stands perfectly still, waiting for a tasty meal to go by. Then it grabs its prey in its spiky forearms and starts to eat.

Big and Beautiful

The morpho is the world's biggest butterfly. Its beautiful, shimmering blue wings can stretch up to 8 inches (20 cm) wide, about the size of a cereal bowl.

morpho

rhino beetle

Weight Lifters

Rhino beetles grow up to 2.5 inches (6.3 cm) long, but they are incredibly strong for their size. They can lift up to 100 times their own weight. That's like a grown man picking up a draft horse!

praying mantis

Deadly Touch

Poison dart frogs are only about 1.9 inches (5 cm) long, but they are the most poisonous creatures in the world. A poison dart frog's body contains enough poison to kill 10 humans. Don't touch!

poison dart frog

Fearsome Fangs

The Amazon giant centipede can grow up to 12 inches (30 cm) long. It hunts for animals on the forest floor and injects them with poison from its fangs.

giant centipede

Forests of Change

There are different things to discover all year round in temperate forests. In autumn, the trees drop their leaves. In spring, they grow new ones, and all kinds of animals begin building their homes.

Spot the Deer

It would be difficult to spot a fallow deer and her fawn in the woods. The deers' coats are speckled, making them hard to see in the mixture of sunlight and shadows beneath the trees.

fallow deer

pine marten

Hidden Harvest

Wood mice live in burrows among the tree roots. They store nuts and berries in their underground home so they won't go hungry in winter.

wood mouse

Secret Squirrels

Squirrels build a tree nest called a drey. It looks like a ball of twigs. The tiny squirrel babies are born inside.

red squirrel

Perfect Pecking

Woodpeckers lay their eggs and hatch their chicks in tree holes that they dig with their sharp beaks.

woodpecker

Cozy Cubs

Fox cubs are born in springtime inside the cozy, safe den their parents have dug. The cubs emerge outside to play once they are big and strong enough.

fox

Hungry Hunters

Life in the forest isn't always peaceful and safe. There are hunters on the prowl, such as pine martens. They catch small creatures, and they steal eggs and chicks, too.

There's an Owl

It's dusk, just before the temperate woods darken into nighttime.
A silver shape is gliding low through the trees. There's an owl overhead!

Hiding Up High

Woodland owls roost among tree branches. They're hard to see because their feathers are speckled.

Spectacular Senses

Owls hunt at dawn and dusk, when the light is low. They have great hearing and eyesight, so they don't need a lot of light to spot their prey.

Silent Swoopers

Owls have specially adapted feathers that muffle the sound of their wing beats. Their prey don't hear them coming.

Look Around

An owl can't move its eyes from side to side, like you can. It must turn its entire head to look around.

Owl Babies

Tawny owls live in the temperate woods of Europe, Asia, and Africa. In springtime, their babies are born in nests inside tree holes.

Fluffy Family

There are usually two or three glossy white eggs in the nest. They hatch into little fluffy chicks.

Little Squeaks

The owl baby will call to its parents with a high squeak. It won't make a hooting noise until it has grown bigger.

tawny owl

First Flight

When a baby is big enough, it will hop out of the nest and learn to jump and flutter. Its parents will feed it until it is finally ready to fly.

Tree-mendous Homes

Some people build their homes among the trees of the world's great forests, and some hunt animals for food, or forage for nuts and fruit.

Comfortable Cabin

This log cabin is deep in the boreal forest in Alaska. Logs are also burned in the fireplace for warmth.

Rooftop Leaves

The roof of this house in Thailand is made from rain forest leaves. The leaves are waterproof, so they help to keep the home dry.

Everyone Inside

This is a rain forest longhouse on the tropical island of Borneo. Many families live in the longhouse, each with their own rooms. Their pigs and chickens live underneath the house.

Treetop Home

Treehouses can be built among the canopies of the trees, like this one in Indonesia. Imagine sleeping as high as the birds!

Touch a Tree

Wood is all around your home. It can make furniture, like tables and chairs, and if you are holding this book, you are touching part of a tree right now. We use trees to make all kinds of things, including paper.

1 Trees are cut down and turned into tiny pieces, called woodchips, to make paper.

2 The woodchips are mixed with water to make mushy pulp, like oatmeal.

3 The pulp goes through a giant paper machine, where it is pressed into thin sheets and dried out.

4 You can recycle paper. It goes back to the paper mill to be pulped and made into clean new sheets.

Grow Again

In a sustainable forest, new trees are planted to replace the ones that are cut down. This helps to keep the planet green.

You are touching something made from wood. Keep it safe. A tree grew it!

Index